THE
Pointless Book

STARTED BY ALFIE DEYES
FINISHED BY YOU

RUNNING PRESS
PHILADELPHIA · LONDON

THE POINTLESS BOOK APP

WATCH ALFIE IN ACTION

SCAN ME

TAKE POINTLESSNESS TO ANOTHER LEVEL WITH THE POINTLESS BOOK APP WITH EXCLUSIVE VIDEOS FROM ALFIE AND MORE! ACCESS THE FREE APP FROM ITUNES OR GOOGLE PLAY, POINT YOUR DEVICE AT THE PAGES WITH THE ICON ABOVE, AND THE VIDEOS WILL BE REVEALED ON SCREEN. HERE YOU WILL GET THE CHANCE TO WATCH VIDEOS OF ALFIE MAKING A CAKE IN A MUG, PLAYING HAND SLAPS AND TAKING PART IN THE VARIOUS FUN CHALLENGES AND ACTIVITIES!

THE POINTLESS BOOK APP REQUIRES AN INTERNET CONNECTION TO BE DOWNLOADED, AND CAN BE USED ON IPHONE, IPAD OR ANDROID DEVICES. FOR DIRECT LINKS TO DOWNLOAD THE APP AND FURTHER INFORMATION, VISIT WWW.RUNNINGPRESS.COM

COMPLETE THIS BOOK IN A POINTLESS ORDER!

MY JOURNAL THIS WEEK

WEEK STARTING ___ / / ___

WRITE DOWN ONE SENTENCE TO DESCRIBE EACH
OF YOUR DAYS THIS WEEK.

MONDAY _____

_____

TUESDAY _____

_____

WEDNESDAY _____

_____

THURSDAY _____

_____

FRIDAY _____

_____

SATURDAY _____

_____

SUNDAY _____

_____

STICK A PHOTO HERE

WRITE DOWN YOUR FAVORITE QUOTE AND WHO SAID IT

SEE
ALFIE'S
QUOTE

SPRAY YOUR FAVORITE SCENT ON THIS PAGE FOR WHEN YOU'RE FEELING DOWN

SMELL ME

WOULD YOU RATHER...

SEE ALFIE'S CHOICES

1) Have wings or fins?

2) Have candy for dinner every day for a month or have a pint of curdled milk?

3) Have no elbows or no knees?

4) Be in a cave of spiders or snakes?

5) Swim with crocodiles or sharks?

6) Drink your own urine or eat your own puke?

7) Fight a horse-sized duck or 100 duck-sized horses?

8) Have legs as long as your fingers or fingers as long as your legs?

9) Be sexually attracted to fruit or have Cheetos dust permanently stuck to your fingers?

10) Speak any language fluently or be able to speak to animals?

WRITE DOWN YOUR TOP FIVE CELEBRITY CRUSHES

(LOOK AT THIS LIST A MONTH FROM NOW AND SEE IF YOU STILL AGREE!)

1.

2.

3.

4.

5.

ORIGAMI TIME!

CUT OUT THIS SQUARE AND FOLLOW THE
INSTRUCTIONS ON THE NEXT PAGE

CUT HERE

CUT HERE

CUT HERE

ORIGAMI TIME!

INSTRUCTIONS:

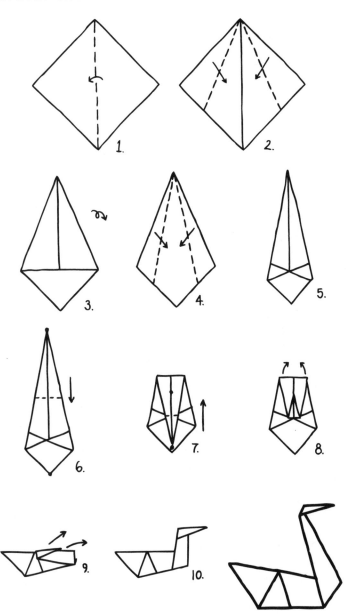

MAKE A PICTURE...

...WITH THE CIRCLE

BUCKET LIST

WRITE DOWN TEN THINGS YOU'D LIKE TO DO BEFORE YOU GET OLD...

1.

2.

3.

4.

5.

6.

7.

8.

9.

10.

TAKE YOUR POINTLESS BOOK ON A DATE...

WHERE DID YOU GO?

_____
_____
_____
_____
_____

WHAT DID YOU TALK ABOUT?

_____
_____
_____
_____

DID YOU KISS?

_____
_____

ACCENTS CHALLENGE

PLAY THE ACCENTS CHALLENGE WITH A FEW FRIENDS! DO YOUR BEST IMPRESSION OF SOMEONE TALKING IN THE FOLLOWING ACCENTS AND ASK YOUR FRIENDS TO GUESS THE COUNTRY:

AUSTRALIAN

JAMAICAN

BRITISH

FRENCH

CHINESE

SCOTTISH

POINTLESS PAGE!

WHEN YOU SEE THIS PAGE FILL IT IN WITH WHATEVER YOU WANT!

DRAW THE HAIR!

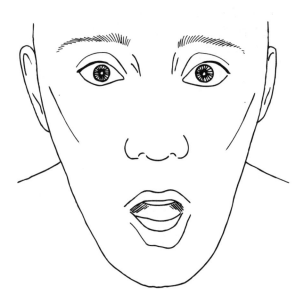

DRAW THE HAT!

DRAW SOME MAKE UP...

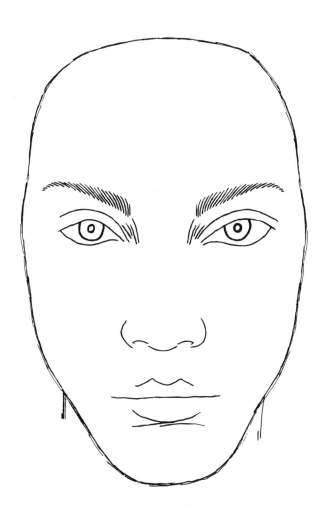

SPOT THE DIFFERENCE...

...FIVE DIFFERENCES TO FIND!

BEIGHTON PIER

DREAM JOURNAL

LAST NIGHT I DREAMT: _____

_____

_____

_____

_____

_____

_____

_____

_____

_____

_____

_____

_____

_____

_____

_____

I THINK THIS MEANS: _____

_____

_____

_____

_____

_____

_____

Write a message for a friend and swap pages with them...

TEAR HERE

TAKE A BITE OUT
OF THIS PAGE

FAVORITE EVER...

(LOOK BACK IN A MONTH AND UPDATE!)

BOOK: _____

_____

SONG: _____

_____

COLOR: _____

_____

YOUTUBER: _____

_____

FRIEND: _____

_____

BLOGGER: _____

_____

VIDEO GAME: _____

_____

FILM: _____

_____

WEBSITE: _____

EAT SOME DRY CRACKERS...

HOW MANY CAN YOU GET IN YOUR
MOUTH AT ONCE?

_____

HOW FAST CAN YOU EAT
ONE CRACKER?

_____

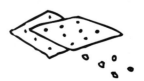

THE DICE GAME

CUT OUT THE PAPER CUBE TEMPLATE ON THE OPPOSITE
PAGE, FOLD ON THE LINES AND TAPE TOGETHER TO MAKE
THE DICE!

WRITE DOWN SIX THINGS THAT YOU **HAVE** TO DO IF YOU
ROLL THE DICE ON THAT NUMBER. IT CAN BE A DARE, A GOOD
DEED, ANYTHING, BUT YOU HAVE TO DO IT!

CUT OUT THE DICE TEMPLATE
(JUST THE OUTLINE)

FOLD

FOLD

FOLD

FOLD

FOLD

FOLD

FOLD

FOLD

FOLD

(YOU WILL NEED STICKY TAPE!)

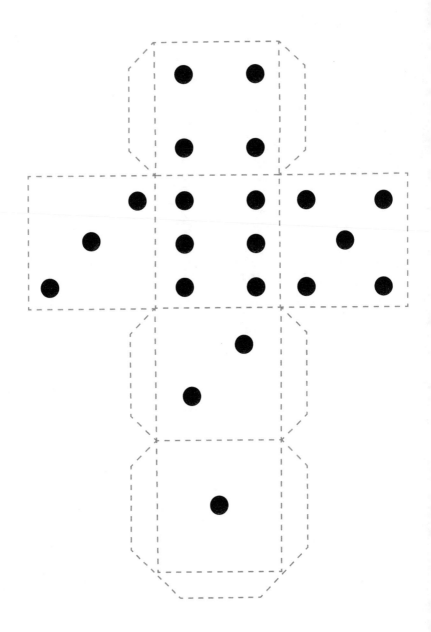

PLAY HAND-SLAPS

SCAN HERE

KEEP SCORE HERE:

PLAYER 1	PLAYER 2

WINNER: _____

DESIGN A TATTOO
DRAW A TATTOO YOU'D LOVE TO GET IN THE FUTURE

STAPLE THIS PAGE

CREATE SOME ART
#THEPOINTLESSBOOK
WITH YOUR DESIGN

PEOPLE-WATCHING PAGE...

Tick when you see:

☐ A MAN WITH A BEARD

☐ A LADY WITH RED HAIR

☐ SOMEONE WEARING A CAST

☐ A CHILD WITH A PACIFIER

☐ A YELLOW CAR

☐ SOMEONE TAKING A SELFIE

☐ A MAILMAN

DRAW THESE SHAPES...

...WITHOUT TAKING YOUR PEN OFF THE PAPER

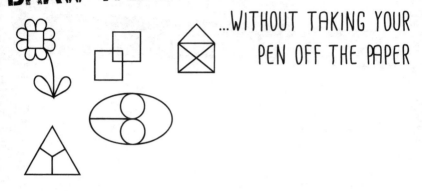

CONSEQUENCES...

FOLD HERE

...INSTRUCTIONS OVERLEAF

CONSEQUENCES...

PLAY WITH A FRIEND!

1. WRITE DOWN A GIRL'S NAME, FOLD IT OVER AND HAND TO THE NEXT PLAYER.

2. WRITE A BOY'S NAME, FOLD IT OVER AND PASS ON AGAIN.

3. WRITE WHERE THEY MET, FOLD OVER AND PASS ON.

4. WRITE WHAT SHE SAID TO HIM, FOLD OVER AND PASS ON.

5. WRITE WHAT HE SAID TO HER.

6. CONSEQUENCE...YOU DECIDE THE ENDING.

7. UNRAVEL THE STORY AND READ BACK!

WRITE DOWN YOUR FIVE FAVORITE THINGS ABOUT YOURSELF AND WHY...

1.

2.

3.

4.

5.

PASS YOUR BOOK TO A STRANGER AND ASK THEM TO DRAW A PICTURE OF YOU...

WORD SEARCH!

B	O	Y	O	U	T	U	B	E	A	P	T	A	Q	R
F	I	R	B	V	B	T	S	X	H	C	B	C	H	P
O	N	D	V	J	R	S	E	W	P	O	H	S	G	O
T	K	J	K	G	M	K	W	N	Y	F	K	K	P	I
R	S	N	T	I	J	Y	S	D	R	F	C	V	S	N
A	M	J	L	Y	N	T	V	R	M	E	R	J	B	T
V	G	E	L	P	R	I	E	H	B	E	T	J	R	L
E	R	L	G	L	M	G	T	N	Q	Z	D	N	B	E
L	V	S	X	U	G	C	U	S	R	T	Z	K	I	S
E	D	U	T	O	W	F	B	Y	D	E	W	E	C	S
M	O	V	L	S	Z	G	T	H	I	U	L	U	F	B
L	N	V	O	P	L	H	B	R	E	F	Y	H	R	O
D	C	S	G	N	I	W	N	E	K	C	I	H	C	O
T	H	T	P	O	C	D	G	W	N	F	C	K	O	K
B	R	I	G	H	T	O	N	X	S	S	F	N	Y	S

YOUTUBE   SMILE   COFFEE

VLOGGER   BRIGHTON   INTERNET

POINTLESS BOOK   TRAVEL   CHICKEN WINGS

TRACE THE OUTLINE OF YOUR FAVORITE FOOD ON THIS PAGE...

CONCERTINA STORY

WRITE A COUPLE OF LINES OF A STORY, FOLD BACK THE PAGE FOR A FRIEND TO
WRITE THE NEXT LINE AND SO ON... OPEN UP TO REVEAL A HILARIOUS STORY

FOLD HERE

...IRON THE CREASES OUT OF THIS PAGE.

PLAY A SONG AND WRITE THE LYRICS ON THIS PAGE...

DRAW CLOTHES ON THE PEOPLE BELOW...

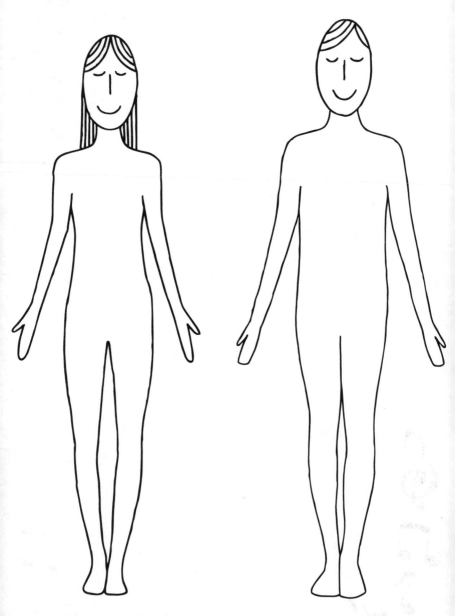

WRITE A COMPLIMENT ON
THIS PAGE, RIP IT OUT
AND PASS IT TO A FRIEND

TAKE A PHOTO OF YOURSELF HOLDING YOUR
BOOK IN THE CRAZIEST PLACE YOU CAN
THINK OF AND UPLOAD IT USING

#PBONTOUR

MAKE THIS PAGE AS MESSY AS YOU CAN

ALFIE'S CAKE IN A MUG RECIPE...

WATCH ALFIE IN ACTION

INGREDIENTS

4 TBSP SELF-RISING FLOUR

2 TBSP COCOA POWDER

4 TBSP SUGAR

3 TBSP MILK

1 MEDIUM EGG

3 TBSP VEGETABLE/ SUNFLOWER OIL

A FEW DROPS VANILLA EXTRACT (IF YOU'RE FEELING FANCY)

2 TBSP CHOCOLATE CHIPS

METHOD

FIND A MUG. MAKE SURE IT'S A BIG ONE OTHERWISE IT'LL OVERFLOW IN THE MICROWAVE. PLUS WE ALL LIKE A BIG CAKE

ADD THE FLOUR, COCOA POWDER AND SUGAR TO THE MUG AND MIX INTO A CHOCOLATY PASTE. ADD THE EGG AND GIVE IT A GOOD MIX; THEN ADD EVERYTHING ELSE — SO THE MILK, VEGETABLE OIL AND THE VANILLA ESSENCE — BUT NOT THE CHOCOLATE CHIPS! ONCE YOU HAVE EVERYTHING IN THE MUG AND IT'S LOOKING SMOOTH AND DELICIOUS, ADD THE CHOCOLATE CHIPS.

PLACE YOUR LOVELY MUG IN THE MIDDLE OF THE MICROWAVE AND COOK ON THE HIGHEST SETTING FOR 4-5 MINUTES. KEEP AN EYE ON IT THROUGH THE WINDOW AS IT MIGHT OVERFLOW.

WAIT FOR THE 'DING'. TAKE THE MUG OUT, LET IT COOL THEN SIT DOWN AND EAT!

REMEMBER
TO DRINK
LOTS OF
WATER
TODAY.
STAY
HYDRATED
:)

WRITE WHATEVER'S ON YOUR MIND

...WITHOUT STOPPING UNTIL YOU GET TO THE END OF THE PAGE

DRAW YOUR OWN
TIME MACHINE

DRAW WHERE YOU'D LIKE TO GO—TO THE PAST OR THE FUTURE?

POINTLESS PAGE!

WHEN YOU SEE THIS PAGE FILL IT IN WITH WHATEVER YOU WANT!

A TEAR-OFF LETTER

WRITE SOMEONE YOU KNOW A LETTER ON THIS
PIECE OF PAPER, TEAR IT OFF AND SEND IT TO THEM

- -

TEAR HERE

DOT
TO
DOT!

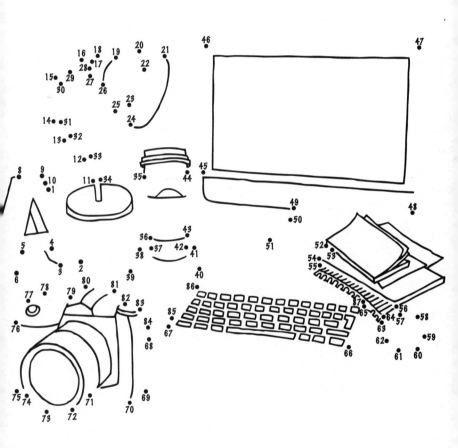

BURY THIS BOOK UNDERGROUND

(FOR ONE NIGHT, DIG IT UP AND SIGN THIS PAGE ONCE YOU'VE DONE SO.)

DATE: _____

SIGN HERE: _____

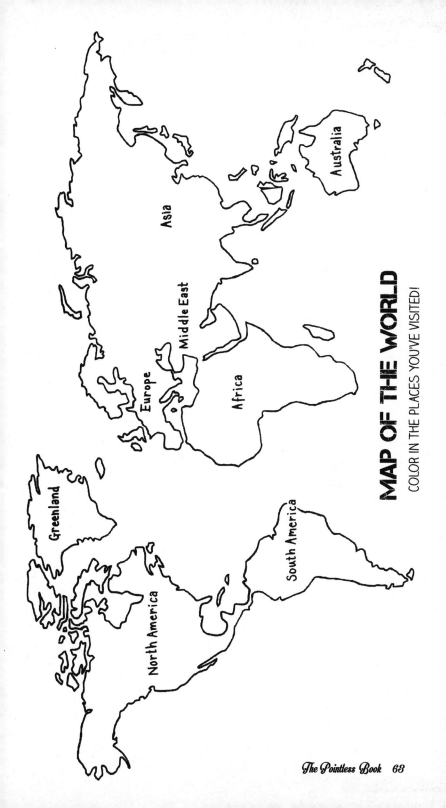

MAP OF THE WORLD

COLOR IN THE PLACES YOU'VE VISITED!

Greenland

North America

South America

Europe

Middle East

Africa

Asia

Australia

MY LIFE AMBITIONS...

IN MY LIFE I WOULD LIKE TO...

1.

2.

3.

4.

5.

6.

PAPER AIRPLANE COMPETITION

RIP OUT THIS PAGE AND MAKE A PAPER AIRPLANE.

TEAR OUT

② FOLD

② FOLD

① FOLD

TEAR OUT

FOLD ③

FOLD ③

FOLD ⑤

FOLD ⑤

FOLD ④

FIVE YOGA POSITIONS TO LEARN...

COBRA

FIVE YOGA POSITIONS TO LEARN...

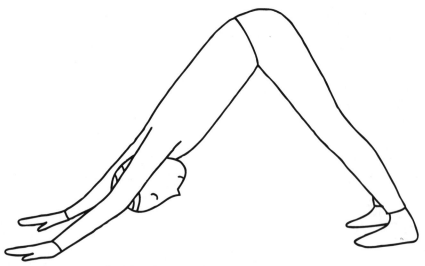

DOWNWARD-FACING DOG

WATCH
ALFIE IN
ACTION

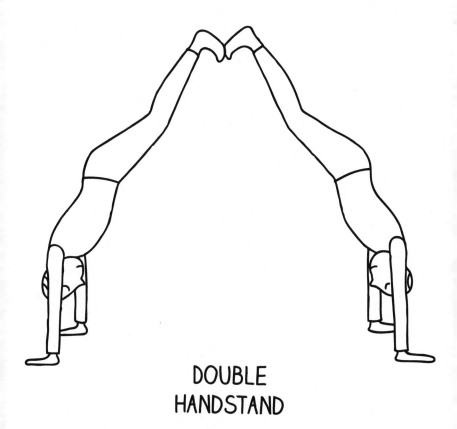

DOUBLE
HANDSTAND

FIVE YOGA POSITIONS TO LEARN...

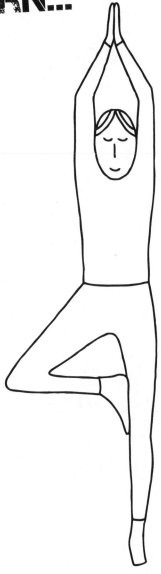

TREE

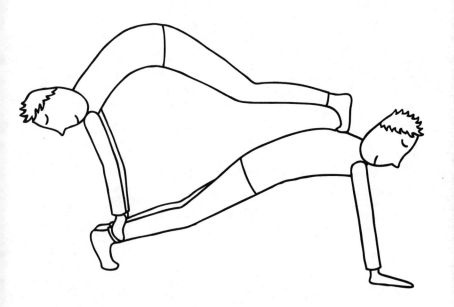

DOUBLE
TRIANGLE

GO TO PAGE 97

GO TO PAGE 97

MESSAGE IN A BOOK...

WRITE A MESSAGE ON THIS PAGE, RIP IT OUT AND SNEAK IT
INTO SOMEONE ELSE'S BOOK!

TEAR HERE

IF YOU'RE LUCKY ENOUGH TO FIND THIS PAGE TWEET
#THEPOINTLESSBOOK

#THEPOINTLESSBOOK

DRAW A FINGER SELFIE...

PLACE A FINGER IN ONE OF THE SPACES BELOW AND DRAW A FACE, A BEARD, A CRAZY MOUSTACHE, WHATEVER YOU LIKE AND THERE YOU GO — YOU HAVE A FINGER SELFIE! SHARE YOUR FINGER SELFIES BY POSTING WITH #PBFINGERSELFIE

PLACES I'D LIKE TO TRAVEL TO...

PLAY SQUARES...

...WITH A FRIEND. TAKE TURNS MAKING A LINE JOINING TWO DOTS BUT TRY TO PREVENT THE OTHER PLAYER FROM MAKING A SQUARE. FILL THE DOTS WITH SQUARES AND THE PERSON WITH THE MOST WINS!

MY FAVORITE CHILDHOOD MEMORY IS...

SEE
ALFIE'S
MEMORY

GRAFFITI THIS WALL

TURN THIS PAGE WITH YOUR ELBOW

WHAT IS THE LAST THING YOU DO BEFORE YOU FALL ASLEEP AND WHY?

TURN THIS PAGE WITH YOUR EAR

FLICK SOME PAINT ON THIS PAGE

BASKETBALL CHALLENGE

CRUMPLE UP THIS PAGE AND THROW PAPER IN A TRASH CAN.

FINISH OFF THE PICTURE...

NOT TO DO LIST...

WRITE DOWN FIVE THINGS YOU'D LIKE TO AVOID DOING TODAY:

1.

2.

3.

4.

5.

WRITE DOWN A SECRET...

ROAD TRIP!

First one to see a:...

RED CAR ☐

GAS STATION ☐

CROW ☐

TIRE ON THE SIDE OF THE ROAD ☐

GIRL WITH BLONDE HAIR ☐

GUY WEARING A BLUE T-SHIRT ☐

HITCHHIKER ☐

SEAGULL ☐

ROAD KILL ☐

FOOD TRUCK ☐

THE HEADBAND CHALLENGE

Rip out and write down the name of a famous person on the strips below. You and a friend lick and stick it on your head (don't look!) and each person asks a 'yes' or 'no' question in order to guess who their person is.

TEAR HERE

TEAR HERE

TEAR HERE

TEAR HERE

TEAR HERE

TEAR HERE

TEAR HERE

TEAR HERE

DO SOMETHING YOU'VE NEVER DONE BEFORE AND WRITE IT DOWN HERE.

DRAW YOUR DAY IN A STORYBOARD

DRAW HERE

WRITE HERE

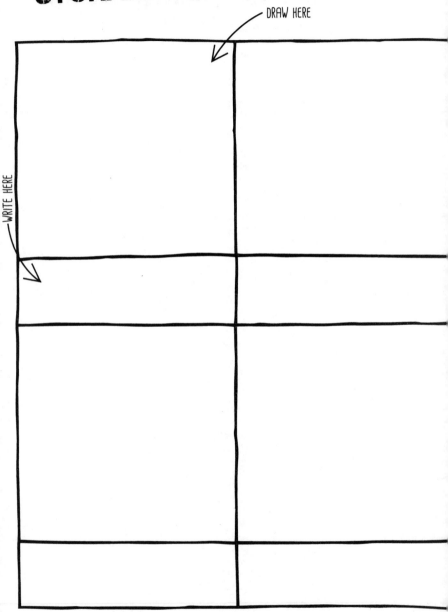

DATE: _____/_____/_____

PASS THIS BOOK...

...WITH A GROUP OF FRIENDS
PASS THE BOOK UNDER YOUR
CHIN, WHOEVER DROPS IT IS OUT!

CHALLENGE TIME

OK, LET'S SEE HOW LONG YOU CAN BE SILENT FOR...

ATTEMPT 1: _____

ATTEMPT 2: _____

ATTEMPT 3: _____

ATTEMPT 4: _____

ATTEMPT 5: _____

PERSONAL BEST: _____

PRESS SOME FLOWERS...

...BETWEEN THESE PAGES

PAINT A PICTURE USING PAINT AND ONLY YOUR FINGERS...

LOVE LETTER...

...TEAR THIS PAGE OUT AND WRITE SOMEONE A LOVE LETTER

TEAR HERE

FOLD IN HALF HERE

PHONE BINGO!

Play Phone Bingo with a friend (or group of friends). Call a random person in your contacts and each player has to get the selected list of words below into the conversation, cross them off, then shout 'Phone Bingo!'

GIRAFFE

SHOELACE

CHICKEN WING

UNICYCLE

EAR WAX

USE YOUR OLD NAIL POLISH TO PAINT THIS PAGE

POINTLESS PAGE!

WHEN YOU SEE THIS PAGE FILL IT IN WITH WHATEVER YOU WANT!

WRITE DOWN WHATEVER YOU DID ON THE PREVIOUS PAGE AND THE REASON WHY YOU DID IT

_____

_____

_____

_____

_____

_____

_____

_____

_____

_____

_____

_____

_____

_____

MUSIC MAKER!

WRITE A SELECTION OF LYRICS FROM YOUR TOP
FIVE FAVORITE SONGS AND MAKE UP A NEW SONG:

HEAD, BODY AND TAILS

WITH A GROUP OF FRIENDS, TAKE IT IN TURN TO DRAW THE PARTS OF A PERSON ON THE PAGE BELOW. BEGIN WITH THE HEAD, FOLD THE PAGE AND PASS TO WHOEVER IS ON YOUR RIGHT. ONCE YOU'VE COMPLETED THE HEAD, SHOULDERS, BODY, LEGS AND FEET, OPEN IT UP TO REVEAL YOUR CREATION!

HEAD

SHOULDERS

TEAR HERE

BODY

LEGS

FEET

ANAGRAM PAGE!

Un-scramble the following Pointless anagrams:

GOBLIN TOPLESS

_____

EARN DUVET

_____

MIMES MUTER

_____

HAT PAY SPY

_____

HAPPY HOG ROT

_____

WRITE A POEM...

BRAIN TEASERS...

TRY YOUR BEST TO SOLVE THESE:

WHAT
TRAVELS
AROUND THE WORLD
BUT STAYS IN THE
CORNER? _____

WHAT GETS
WETTER AND
WETTER THE MORE
IT DRIES? _____

WHAT CAN
YOU CATCH
BUT CAN'T
_____ THROW?

WHICH WORD IN
THE DICTIONARY
IS SPELLED
INCORRECTLY? _____

YOU CAN
HOLD IT WITHOUT
USING YOUR
ARMS. WHAT IS
_____ IT?

NOTES

USE THIS PAGE WHEN YOU NEED SOME PAPER!

POINTLESS PAGE!

WHEN YOU SEE THIS PAGE FILL IT IN WITH WHATEVER YOU WANT!

TURN TO PAGE 15

DESIGN YOUR OWN
ALBUM COVER

MY JOURNAL
THIS WEEK

WEEK STARTING ____/__/____

WRITE DOWN ONE SENTENCE TO DESCRIBE EACH DAY THIS WEEK.

MONDAY _____

_____

TUESDAY _____

_____

WEDNESDAY _____

_____

THURSDAY _____

_____

FRIDAY _____

_____

SATURDAY _____

_____

SUNDAY _____

_____

CONSEQUENCES...

GAME 1:

(SEE RULES ON PAGE 40)

FOLD HERE

GAME 2:

FOLD HERE

TEAR THE CORNERS OFF THIS PAGE

404 PAGE NOT FOUND

HOLE-PUNCH THIS PAGE!

CREATE SOME ART USING A HOLE-PUNCH!

ROCK, PAPER, SCISSORS

SCAN HERE

KEEP SCORE HERE:

PLAYER 1	PLAYER 2

WINNER:

_____

DRAW AROUND YOUR OWN HAND...

THUMB WARS

KEEP SCORE HERE:

PLAYER 1	PLAYER 2

WINNER: _____

PEOPLE WATCHING PAGE...

TICK WHEN YOU SEE:

☐ SOMEONE WEARING FLIP-FLOPS

☐ SOMEONE RIDING A SKATEBOARD

☐ TOO MUCH PDA (PUBLIC DISPLAY OF AFFECTION)

☐ SOMEONE WEARING A BANDANA

☐ SOMEONE RUNNING FOR A BUS

☐ A TREE TALLER THAN YOUR HOUSE

TURN THIS PAGE WITH YOUR NOSE

TURN TO PAGE 190

DOODLE

FILL THIS PAGE WITH DOODLES

HEAD TENNIS

LOOK RIGHT!

$\longrightarrow$

←

LOOK LEFT!

DRAW YOUR WEEK IN A STORYBOARD

DRAW HERE

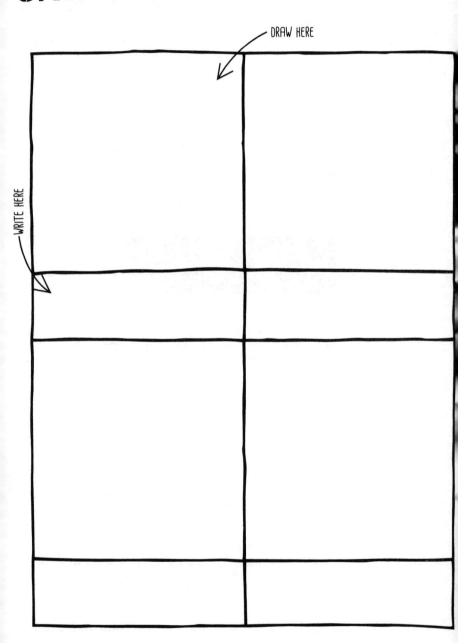

WRITE HERE

F-TEST!

COUNT EVERY "F" IN THE FOLLOWING TEXT

FUNNY FRIENDS ARE
THE RESULT OF YEARS
OF SCIENTIFIC STUDY
COMBINED WITH THE
EXPERIENCE OF YEARS...

WRITE WHAT YOU DID TODAY

...WITH YOUR OPPOSITE WRITING HAND

WHAT'S THE FIRST THING YOU DO IN THE MORNING AND WHY?

POINTLESS PAGE!

WHEN YOU SEE THIS PAGE FILL IT IN WITH WHATEVER YOU WANT!

RANDOM TWEET!

WHENEVER YOU OPEN
THE BOOK OR PASS
THIS PAGE YOU HAVE TO
TWEET SOMETHING WITH

#THEPOINTLESSBOOK

DRAW A 'SELFIE'

TIME CAPSULE

PUT SOMETHING BETWEEN THESE TWO PAGES
AND GLUE THEM TOGETHER. WRITE A DATE ON
THE NEXT PAGE AND DO NOT OPEN UNTIL THEN.

DO NOT OPEN THIS CAPSULE UNTIL

DRAW YOUR PET

(IF YOU DON'T HAVE A PET DRAW A GOLDFISH!)

WITH A FRIEND SEE HOW LONG YOU CAN DIP A COOKIE IN YOUR CUP OF MILK BEFORE IT BREAKS OFF

KEEP SCORE HERE:

YOU	FRIEND

WRITE DOWN SOME FUNNY OVERHEARD CONVERSATIONS...

DRAW A LANDMARK...

...FROM A PLACE YOU WOULD LIKE TO VISIT

CRAZY COCKTAIL

MAKE THE WEIRDEST COCKTAIL POSSIBLE! JOT DOWN
WHAT YOU'VE PUT IN IT (KETCHUP, MUSTARD...) AND
RATE HOW IT TASTED OUT OF 10.

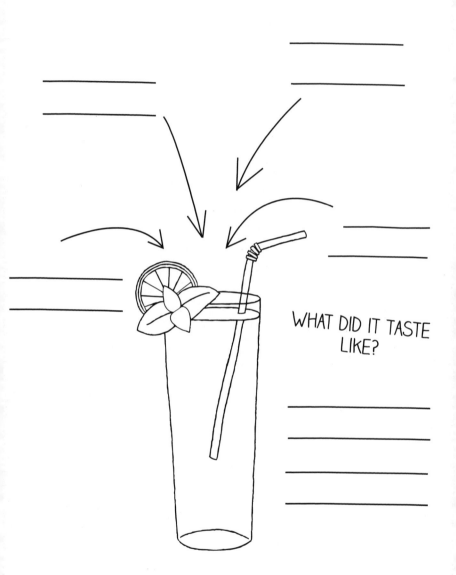

WHAT DID IT TASTE
LIKE?

MAKE A FACE USING MAGAZINE CUT-OUTS...

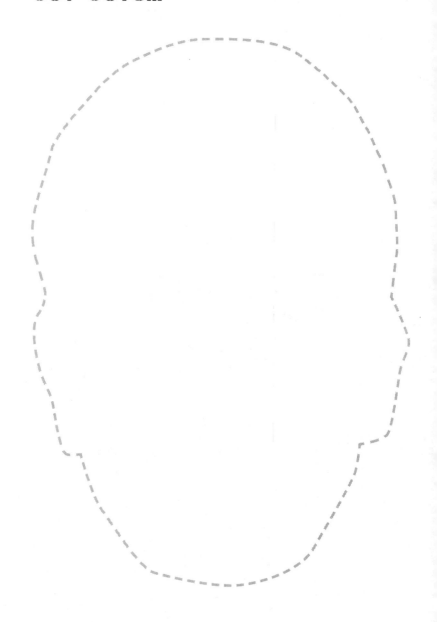

MAKE A SMOOTHIE FROM WHATEVER YOU HAVE IN THE FRIDGE...

INGREDIENTS:

_____

_____

_____

_____

_____

_____

_____

_____

_____

_____

_____

_____

_____

_____

_____

_____

_____

WHAT DID IT TASTE LIKE?

LIST YOUR TOP FIVE FILMS

1.

2.

3.

4.

5.

MY FIRST...

1. WORD

2. FRIEND

3. PET

4. KISS

5. FEAR

6. JOB

7. PHONE

STICK A PHOTO HERE OF WHEN
YOU WERE YOUNG

DRAW WHAT YOU'D LIKE TO BE
WHEN YOU'RE OLDER

ON THE BOARD BELOW WRITE DOWN THE NAME OF FOUR PEOPLE
(TWO YOU LIKE, TWO YOU DISLIKE), FOUR COUNTRIES, AND FOUR
RANDOM NUMBERS. GRAB A PEN AND TAP INSIDE THE BOX UNTIL
A NOMINATED PLAYER SAYS 'STOP!' COUNT THE DOTS AND,
BEGINNING WITH 'M', USE THIS NUMBER TO CROSS OFF THE ANSWERS
SURROUNDING THE BOX, CROSSING OFF AN ANSWER EVERY TIME YOU
GET TO YOUR NUMBER. THE GAME IS COMPLETE WHEN ONE ANSWER
REMAINS IN EACH PANEL...

MASH

MANSION   APARTMENT   SHED   HOUSE

NAMES

COUNTRIES

KIDS

STICK CHEWING GUM
HERE AND FOLD THE CORNER

WHAT DID I DO ON THIS DAY...?

NEW YEAR'S DAY _____

_____

_____

EASTER MONDAY _____

_____

_____

ST PATRICK'S DAY _____

_____

_____

FOURTH OF JULY _____

_____

_____

HALLOWEEN _____

_____

_____

WHO WOULD YOU INVITE TO YOUR DREAM DINNER PARTY?

...CHOOSE ANYONE YOU LIKE, DEAD OR ALIVE.

WOULD YOU RATHER...

1) Be boiling hot or freezing cold?

2) Have your computer memory wiped or have your past and future web browsing history available to everyone?

3) Drink a cup of swimming pool water or sea water?

4) Hiccup for the rest of your life or feel like you have to sneeze but can't for the rest of your life?

5) Listen to one song for the rest of your life or never listen to the same song twice?

6) Not be able to use the internet or not be able to listen to music?

KISS, MARRY, AVOID...

KISS ☐

MARRY ☐

AVOID ☐

_____

KISS ☐

MARRY ☐

AVOID ☐

_____

KISS ☐

MARRY ☐

AVOID ☐

_____

DESCRBE YOURSELF IN FIVE WORDS...

USE THIS PAGE
WHEN YOU
DESPERATELY NEED
A PAPER TOWEL

...DON'T FORGET TO FLUSH...

TURN THIS PAGE WITH YOUR TOE

WHEN YOU SEE THIS PAGE FILL IT IN WITH WHATEVER YOU WANT!

POINTLESS PAGE!

DID THEY:

1. LAUGH
2. CRY
3. THROW UP
4. RUN AWAY

ANAGRAM ANSWERS

GOBLIN TOPLESS

POINTLESS BLOG

EARN DUVET

ADVENTURE

MIMES MUTER

SUMMER TIME

HAT PAY SPY

STAY HAPPY

HAPPY HOG ROT

PHOTOGRAPHY

BRAIN-TEASER ANSWERS

WHAT TRAVELS AROUND THE WORLD BUT STAYS IN THE CORNER?

A POSTAGE STAMP

WHAT GETS WETTER AND WETTER THE MORE IT DRIES?

A TOWEL

WHAT CAN YOU CATCH BUT CAN'T THROW?

A COLD

WHICH WORD IN THE DICTIONARY IS SPELLED INCORRECTLY?

INCORRECTLY

YOU CAN HOLD IT WITHOUT USING YOUR ARMS. WHAT IS IT?

YOUR BREATH

WRITE FIVE THINGS YOU LIKE BEST ABOUT YOURSELF AND WHY...

1. _____
_____
_____
_____

2. _____
_____
_____
_____

3. _____
_____
_____

4. _____
_____
_____

5. _____
_____
_____
_____

SCRAP PAPER...

...USE THIS PAGE WHEN
YOU NEED SOME PAPER

CREATE SOME ART HERE WITH THE HOLES FROM THE HOLE-PUNCH PAGE!

(FROM PAGE 123)

BASKETBALL CHALLENGE

CRUMPLE UP THIS PAGE AND THROW PAPER IN A TRASH CAN.

TOP FIVE THINGS...

...THAT MAKE YOU WANT TO THROW UP.

1. _____

2. _____

3. _____

4. _____

5. _____

CUT OUT NEWSPAPER HEADLINES...

...AND MAKE A STORY HERE!

WRITE A COMPLIMENT...

...RIP OUT THIS PAGE AND GIVE IT TO A STRANGER.

FILL THIS PAGE

WITH THINGS YOU LOVE...

WORD SEARCH ANSWERS...

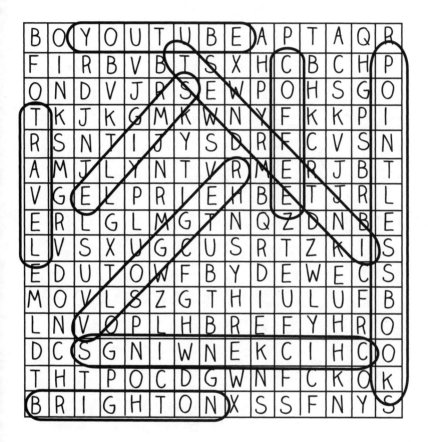

B	O	Y	O	U	T	U	B	E	A	P	T	A	Q	R
F	I	R	B	V	B	T	S	X	H	C	B	C	H	P
O	N	D	V	J	R	S	E	W	P	O	H	S	G	O
T	K	J	K	G	M	K	W	N	Y	F	K	K	P	I
R	S	N	T	I	J	Y	S	D	R	F	C	V	S	N
A	M	J	L	Y	N	T	V	R	M	E	R	J	B	T
V	G	E	L	P	R	I	E	H	B	E	T	R	R	L
E	R	L	G	L	M	G	T	N	Q	Z	D	N	B	E
L	V	S	X	U	G	C	U	S	R	T	Z	K	I	S
E	D	U	T	O	W	F	B	Y	D	E	W	E	C	S
M	O	V	L	S	Z	G	T	H	I	U	L	U	F	B
L	N	V	O	P	L	H	B	R	E	F	Y	H	R	O
D	C	S	G	N	I	W	N	E	K	C	I	H	C	O
T	H	T	P	O	C	D	G	W	N	F	C	K	O	K
B	R	I	G	H	T	O	N	X	S	S	F	N	Y	S

YOUTUBE   SMILE   COFFEE

VLOGGER   BRIGHTON   INTERNET

POINTLESS BOOK   TRAVEL   CHICKEN WINGS

BALANCE THE BOOK ON YOUR HEAD CHALLENGE!

Instructions:

1. Close your Pointless book (not now—wait until you've read all of the instructions first!).

2. Stand in an open space and make sure there aren't any obstacles in your way.

3. Place the book on the middle of your head and take a step forward.

How many steps can you take?

Tweet your best time to #THEPOINTLESSBOOK

TURN TO PAGE 34

DRAW THE HYBRID ANIMALS

DRAW THESE HYBRID ANIMALS: A ZEDONKEY, A GORILLAROO, A CABBIT AND A FROGODILE!

A GEEP

CELEBRITY FISH NAME GAME

FILL THESE PAGES WITH AS MANY CELEBRITY FISH NAMES YOU AND YOUR FRIENDS CAN THINK OF! HERE ARE A FEW TO START YOU OFF:

TUNA TURNER

MUSSEL CROWE

CALAMARI DIAZ

GIVE THIS BOOK TO A FRIEND...

...AND ASK THEM TO DESCRIBE YOU IN THREE WORDS:

DOODLE
TIME!

TURN TO PAGE 130

UGGEST MORE WAYS THIS BOOK CAN BE POINTLESS.
LL OUT THE BOXES BELOW AND SEND IT TO THE ADDRESS
ERLEAF...

1.

2.

3.

4.

5.

6.

RUNNING PRESS

2300 CHESTNUT STREET,

SUITE 200

PHILADEPHIA, PA 19103

U.S.A.